Bridge Builders Mentoring:

Improving Social Mobility and Employability for Young Males

Clive Lewis OBE DL

"Men build too many walls and not enough bridges."

— Isaac Newton

Table of Contents

Author's Note

The publication of this book would not have been possible without the help of some great people. In particular, Amber Bullingham read, re-read, edited and re-edited the manuscript countless times. For her conscientiousness I am highly grateful. I am also indebted to Dame Janet Trotter DBE for her wise counsel and advice during the preparation of this guide. She has helped ensure that the book is rightly balanced for the reader. Finally, I am grateful to Mike Nigro and Leigh Lafever-Ayer at Enterprise Rent-A-Car for partnering with the scheme from day one. Having them by our side in the development of this project has been invaluable.

Thank you for reading.

Clive Lewis OBE DL

Author

Preface

I was born into a working class family. Both of my parents, despite having considerable ability, had to leave school at 14 because of their family circumstances and immediately entered the workforce. Yet I have been incredibly blessed! Both my parents wanted their daughters to fulfil their potential, although they would not have expressed it in these terms. They provided love, stability and encouragement. What we lacked in material possessions they made up for in the richness of love and time.

As I have developed my career I have also been fortunate in having mentors who encouraged, advised, invested time and believed in me: teachers, a Director of ICI, a Jewish rabbi who had been in Auschwitz and professionals from other disciplines - all have helped me to see things in new ways and have contributed to my development.

I am, however, aware that many young people today are inhibited from developing their potential. It may be through family circumstances, grinding poverty, ill-health, caring responsibilities or just not having the right encouragement at the right time.

I believe that as a society we must invest in all of our young people, whatever their circumstances. To achieve a society where all have a valued place it is important for teachers, businesses and individuals to come together to help create a generation which is fully inclusive and where the talents of all are both developed and harnessed. The task is not an easy one. We can, however, help to change perspectives by working together on 'wicked' problems. I commend the Bridge Builders project to you and hope you will find your involvement personally enriching and rewarding.

I am delighted, therefore, to endorse this book and the work of Clive Lewis and Bridge Builders.

Dame Janet Trotter DBE

Introduction

'Education is the most powerful weapon we can use to change the world.'

Nelson Mandela

I am the youngest of five children, born into a family from a poor socio-economic background. My parents emigrated from the Caribbean Island of Jamaica to England in the early 1960s. My dad was a bus driver for most of his career prior to becoming a church minister; my mum was a factory worker. We didn't have much economically. For example, we never experienced a traditional family summer holiday. Excitement for us as children was meeting my dad at the end of the road and climbing on board his bus to ride around with him for a few hours. Fortunately, we were rich in so many other ways.

I was born into a poor socio-economic family, but we were rich in many other ways.

There was no family history of going to university; I left school shortly before my 16th birthday. I followed the trend that had been set. My first job was washing cars. I washed vehicles such as Talbot Horizons and Sunbeams. Every day was the same. After a few months I moved to a new job working at a monastery which had a pottery factory. My job was to put sticky transfers on plates and cups before they were put in the kiln to be fired. In the run up to Christmas of 1985 I got my big break. I was offered a Christmas job in a warehouse at Dixons. Essentially, I spent two months humping boxes around. But I loved the job, and put everything I could into it even going in on my day off to check

I left school at 16 and started work washing cars, before leaving for a job putting sticky transfers onto pottery.

3

on the tidiness of my TV and microwave boxes. My boss liked me. Shortly into the New Year I was offered a full-time job working on the sales floor. Within two years I was promoted to Assistant Manager. A few days before my 19th birthday I was promoted again. This time to Manager of a £1m high street store in Stroud, Gloucestershire.

I found a temporary Christmas job in Dixons warehouse, which led to full time work and, through successive promotions, a store manager role.

People were believing in me. I was getting on with customers, colleagues and management. The interest from others grew and I kept getting promoted. Then, without warning, my career was hit hard. I was asked to take a sideways move and work with a more experienced manager for a while. It was a painful experience at the time. However, it took me on a journey that transformed my life. This happened for two reasons. First, far from becoming my nemesis, my new manager acted as a mentor. He taught me many new skills about running a business and managing people. Such was his impact I still buy him a bottle of his favourite malt whisky for Christmas – nearly 20 years later.

I continued to be promoted until I was asked to work under a more senior manager.

This manager became my mentor.

The second reason for my life transformation is that I used the career 'blip' to deepen my education. I became a part-time university student and studied Human Resources Management and Business for five years. This was in my own time and at my own significant personal expense. It is without doubt, one of the best decisions I have ever made. I learnt so many new things and began liaising and networking with people who in normal circumstances I would have no exposure to. To this day, I remember the principles my tutor taught me. Two which immediately come

I used this career 'blip' to deepen my education, enrolling for a part-time university course, a great personal expense in both time and money.

to mind are his encouragement to watch educational programmes such as *The Money Progamme* and to read broadsheet newspapers. I have read *The Sunday Times* every weekend since 1994. I was later to secure more prestigious senior management roles with other organisations which took me all over the world. I am the author of ten books and run my own group of companies.

In a few short paragraphs, you have read the story of how one man from a poor background gradually changed his life circumstances. A combination of steps underpinned by some incredible people who took the time to help and nurture me to work towards achieving my full potential.

Others with a background similar to mine can break through too. This is why I have set up Bridge Builders Mentoring. I say a little more about how Bridge Builders got started in the next chapter. I am particularly interested in breaking the link between educational and career opportunities and family background, helping to build a system where all young people are given a chance to prosper irrespective of their start in life. The challenge of low social mobility has got even tougher for today's children. This is a concern for families and the economic health of the UK as a whole. Whether you are a teacher, careers advisor, careers manager, education professional, head teacher, mentee, mentor or organisation CEO my hope is that my story will inspire you to get involved. Together we can close the attainment gap which exists between those with a background like mine and those from more affluent backgrounds. Please join me on the journey!

I met people and learnt things I would not otherwise have been exposed to.

This course was a stepping stone to greater things, and I am now able to say that I have worked all over the world in prestigious senior management roles and am the author of ten books.

I set up Bridge Builders to allow others to break through as I did.

I am particularly interested in breaking the link between educational and career opportunities and family background.

Background

'Your education is your life. Guard it well.'

Proverbs 4v13

In 2006, I was invited by the late Home Office Minister, Paul Goggins MP to chair a government appointed panel to research and assess the costs of young male underachievement. Our work was later to be called REACH. In what felt like the blink of an eye, I was thrust into the spotlight working with government ministers, civil servants and key community leaders. Three years later when we reported on our work, it received national media coverage. One of the main reasons for this was the compelling business case upon which our report was based. This suggested a cost to the tax payer of £24bn linked to the Criminal Justice System, education and employment. As part of gathering primary research data we visited five locations including London, Manchester and Birmingham. As we engaged with mothers of those in our target group I recall witnessing a sense of hope radiating from them that help was on the way. People from lower socio-economic backgrounds do not have the same opportunities for educational and career success as their wealthier peers. A person growing up in a low income community can get caught up in the cyclical effects of low educational achievement, inferior job opportunities and greatly increased chances of drug use, poor health and involvement with crime. We must change this.

In 2006, I was invited to chair a government appointed panel to research and assess the costs of young male underachievement.

I saw first-hand how easily and quickly those from poor socio-economic backgrounds got into a spiral of social decline and underachievement.

£24 bn { Education
Employment
Criminal Justice
System

Costs of male
underachievement by 2050
as revealed by the REACH
report, 2007

My role as Chair of the REACH Panel ended with the publication of the report. I remained gripped, however, by the issues which had surfaced during the time in which our research was being conducted. At some stage I knew I would return to the agenda to make a contribution to try and stem the ever increasing flow of challenges that affect people from disadvantaged backgrounds.

A second dilemma which has presented itself has been my interaction with youngsters in the workplace. As a small business owner I have sought the assistance of university work placement students on a number of occasions. On balance, I have been significantly less than satisfied with the experiences I have encountered. Out of a total of six placements, only two were able to complete their assignments. I had to cut short the tenure of the others due to a variety of reasons ranging from attitude and time keeping through to an inability to write coherently or hold an adult conversation on the phone with a customer. They were not work ready. When I expressed my concerns with university staff about the trends I was seeing, the organisations seemed

On balance, I have been significantly less than satisfied with the experiences I have encountered when working with young people in the workplace.

Issues I have encountered include poor timekeeping and quality of work and the inability to write coherently or hold an adult conversation with a customer.

powerless to do anything constructive. I began to suspect that something was missing from the curriculum that would help pupils leave with increased chances of being able to secure and retain employment.

I am delighted that there seems to have been a moodswing which recognises that the UK has a problem to face up to. Every year thousands of pupils are leaving school who are not sufficiently equipped for the world of work. An opportunity exists to make a real difference here.

Bridge Builders has a focus on increasing social mobility and employability for males from age 12-30.

The two experiences I highlight above have led me to launch Bridge Builders Mentoring. The scheme has a focus on increasing social mobility and employability for males from age 12-30. I have come across a range of excellent organisations doing similar work for girls. In the remainder of this short guidebook I attempt to set out how the scheme is a toolkit designed to tackle many of the factors holding individuals back from achieving their full potential.

The mentors provided by Bridge Builders are middle and senior managers from large corporate organisations I have worked with in business.

How does Bridge Builders differ?

Mentoring isn't new and I am often asked about the difference with Bridge Builders in comparison to other initiatives. There is one main difference. The mentors provided by Bridge Builders are middle and senior managers from large corporate organisations I have worked with in business. Many of our corporate customers share values similar to those underpinning Bridge Builders. The mentors are instantly credible with the young mentees as they are walking examples of people who have proved their own ability. They are holding down big jobs whilst still finding time to give back to the communities in which they work.

They are holding down big jobs whilst still finding time to give back to the communities in which they work.

Size of the reading gap between high achieving boys from privileged backgrounds and their counterparts from poor families.

The Sutton Trust, 2013 [FF2]

How Does Bridge Builders Work?

'A child without education is like a bird without wings.'

Tibetan proverb

The Bridge Builders Mentoring Scheme specifically targets boys who are eligible for free school meals, 'looked after' or Forces children. The scheme aims to provide these young men with support and guidance to bridge the gap between their low income backgrounds and their real potential.

The Bridge Builders Mentoring Scheme specifically targets boys who are eligible for free school meals, looked after children or Forces children.

The scheme comprises four parts:

We provide schools with all the information, help and advice they might need to implement the Bridge Builders programme, including meetings and presentations to staff and governors, as required.

Schools approach Bridge Builders to run a mentoring scheme for their pupils. We provide schools with all the information, help and advice they might need to implement the programme, including meetings and presentations to staff and governors, as required. Typically, a school will have a cohort of ten to 15 boys they feel will benefit most from having an external mentor and provide Bridge Builders with relevant information. We then contact mentors based in the locality in order to identify those most suitable. Generally, there is a ratio of one mentor to three or four pupils.

The Process

Mentoring takes place on a monthly basis throughout the school year, ten sessions in total, typically lasting the equivalent of a lesson period i.e. 50 to 60 minutes. Additional contact between mentors and mentees can be arranged at the mentors and the school's discretion. Quarterly review meetings with the mentors and school's representative are recommended to ensure that the mentees are getting the most out of the Scheme, and to address any issues that may arise. Towards the end of the initial ten sessions, the school will then decide if continuing mentoring for each individual child would be useful, and liaise with Bridge Builders to make arrangements. If not, the mentor will discuss the closure of the mentoring programme with each mentee, in order to finalise the relationship on a positive note.

Schools play an essential role in the social and personal development of boys into young men. Integrating a mentoring programme into the school lives of pupils from poor socio-economic backgrounds is just one way in which schools can facilitate this development where it is most often needed. At Bridge Builders, we work in partnership with schools to deliver this opportunity. Full support from the school is essential to the viability of each programme.

Mentoring takes place on a monthly basis throughout the school year, ten sessions in total, typically lasting the equivalent of a lesson time.

Towards the end of the initial ten sessions, the school will then decide if continuing mentoring for each individual child would be useful.

At Bridge Builders, we work in partnership with schools to facilitate the transformation of boys into young men.

With this in mind, the role of the school or representative in Bridge Builders includes:

- Providing information on mentees' academic performance, attendance levels, behavioural issues, and any other relevant details prior to, during and at the end of mentoring, for ongoing monitoring and evaluation

- Providing a safe, private area to be used for the sessions.

- Meeting with the mentors before and after sessions to give feedback.

- Additionally, engaging in quarterly meetings with mentors to review the programme and discuss and resolve any issues.

- Supporting the mentors with any issues surrounding bullying, abuse or child protection.

- Ensuring all staff are aware of the importance of the mentoring programme.

We have experienced high success working with dedicated careers managers and advisors. Where a member of teaching staff will be the lead liaison for those on the Bridge Builders Scheme we recommend that support is also provided from a member of administrative, non-teaching staff, on the day of each session. Tasks such as coordinating the mentees to be at the right place and time for their mentoring session can be undertaken by this person. This relieves the pressure where there are potential clashes with teaching commitments.

We have experienced high success working with dedicated careers managers and advisors.

Evaluation

Previous research suggests that school-based mentoring has a multitude of benefits for the mentee such as improved academic performance, higher attendance levels and reduced behavioural issues. Nevertheless, it is important to record and monitor the progress of every mentor and mentee at every school.

Monitoring feedback and progress is an essential part of the Bridge Builders Mentoring Scheme.

Monitoring feedback and progress is an essential part of the Bridge Builders Mentoring Scheme. Before the commencement of each programme we ask each school to provide us with the following data for each mentee:

- Attendance levels (and targets)

- Attainment levels (and targets)

- Merit points (or other award frameworks)

- Behavioural records

- Exclusion or suspension records

This information is confidential, and serves as a means of quantifying the progression of each pupil and the impact the mentoring programme is having upon them. In addition to quantifiable data, schools should also record feedback from teachers, other staff, parents and peers. Changes in attitude or behaviour can be difficult to assess, but they are often the most important changes that can occur as a result of mentoring, and are inextricably linked to the measurable data.

In addition to quantifiable data, schools should also record feedback from teachers, other staff, parents and peers.

Evaluating the success of the Bridge Builders Mentoring Scheme by using these records provides schools with an additional tool for monitoring their funding decisions. Results and feedback from every mentee and every school are essential to ensure our programmes are relevant and continue to evolve successfully.

Results and feedback from every mentee and every school is essential to ensure our programmes are relevant and continue to evolve successfully.

1. Contact Bridge Builders

2. School visit

3. Choose programme

4. Choose pupils

5. Mentors selected

6. Mentors checked and trained by Bridge Builders

7. Monthly sessions at school

8. Ongoing feedback and reviews

9. Closure and evaluation

10. Celebrate success

Over 60% of children on Free School Meals did not achieve 5 A*-C grades at GCSE in 2013

Department of Education, 2014 FF3

Clive Lewis

Mentoring

'Education is the ability to listen to almost anything without losing your temper or self-confidence.'

Robert Frost

School-based mentoring is a flexible, straightforward concept. Pupils benefit from the focused support and guidance of an additional adult in their lives, especially poignant for those from poor socio-economic backgrounds for whom one or more parents are often absent or unable to provide such assistance. For schools, mentoring requires little staff time and occurs on-site during the school day, therefore mentoring programmes are relatively inexpensive and easy to adopt.

The support of the school gives both the pupils and their parents confidence in the scheme, and provides opportunities for many children who otherwise would not be able or willing to access mentoring programmes.

The success of school-based mentoring is widely reported. For example, the biggest mentoring programme in the USA is run by an organisation called Big Brothers Big Sisters America (BBBSA), which helps over 125,000 children nationwide in its school-based programme annually. A report in 2011 of the BBBSA school-based mentoring scheme highlighted the impact of mentoring relationships on the pupils involved[1]. The results were very encouraging. By the end of their first year of mentoring, there were statistically significant improvements in:

School-based mentoring is a flexible, straightforward concept that benefits both the pupil and the school.

Pupils benefit from the focused support and guidance of an additional adult in their lives.

Schools benefit because mentoring programmes are relatively inexpensive and easy to adopt.

- Socio-economic competency (e.g. social acceptance, parental trust)

- Educational success (e.g. scholastic competency, grades)

- Avoidance of behaviours that could negatively affect their futures (e.g. attitude towards drinking, smoking, truancy, violence)

These are undoubtedly all key areas that schools in the UK would also hope to target with mentoring programmes. School-based mentoring is capable of yielding measurable results for the young people it helps. Other studies have recorded substantial improvements in attitude, expression, trust, respect and relationships with adults. The benefits of school-based mentoring are clear, and the Bridge Builders Mentoring Scheme is well positioned to provide schools with the mentors and guidance to implement and integrate an effective mentoring programme that will make a difference.

Studies into school-based mentoring programs have found improvements in attitude, expression, trust, respect and relationships with adults.

Mentoring is considered particularly effective for less advantaged young people. In 2012, a review by the Joseph Rowntree Foundation concluded that "there is promising evidence of mentoring having an impact on both educational attainment and on attitudes and aspirations."[2] In the context of social mobility, mentoring was recognised as an important opportunity for young people from poor socio-economic backgrounds to develop relationships with older, more experienced people. Often, children from privileged backgrounds have the opportunity to do this on a regular, informal basis. In this way, the Joseph Rowntree Foundation

Mentoring is considered particularly effective for less advantaged young people.

considered mentoring to increase the social capital of disadvantaged children by enhancing their social network and experience.

It is important to note, however, that the positive impact of mentoring programmes depends heavily on their design and implementation. In their 2013 review, Gutman and Schoon[3] identified the strength of the relationship between mentee and mentor as the most influencing factor.

Mentoring is a long-standing form of training, learning and development in a one-to-one format – that of 'mentor' and 'mentee'. It has become an increasingly popular tool for supporting personal development, with one of its major advantages being that no formal qualifications are required – anyone can be a mentor if they have something to pass on and the skills, time and commitment to do it.

Traditionally, mentoring is the long-term passing on of support, guidance and advice. Under the Bridge Builders Scheme it is intended to describe a relationship in which a more experienced person uses their greater knowledge and understanding of life and the world of work to support the development of a more junior or inexperienced person. The end result will be to increase the chances of the mentee to fulfil their full potential and enhance their employability; this is the aim of the Bridge Builders Mentoring Scheme, with the mentor helping create a bridge from underachievement to forming and fulfilling ambitions. It is a form of apprenticeship, whereby an inexperienced learner acquires life and career skills from an experienced mentor.

A 2013 review found that the strength of the relationship between mentee and mentor was the most influencing factor in the success of a mentoring programme.

Mentoring is a long-standing form of training, learning and development in a one-to-one format – that of 'mentor' and 'mentee'.

In Bridge Builders, mentoring means a relationship in which a more experienced person uses their greater knowledge and understanding of life and the world of work to support the development of a more junior or inexperienced person.

The objective of mentoring is to reveal some of the otherwise hidden basic principles that would prevent the mentee from progressing. Mentoring is used specifically and independently as a form of long-term tailored development for the individual, with the aim of improving the life chances for both the individual being mentored and their family. Mentoring is essentially a supportive form of development to assist an individual to improve their life skills and ultimately improve their career.

Mentoring is essentially a supportive form of development to assist an individual to improve their life skills and ultimately improve their career.

The format of mentoring programmes varies widely, depending on the individual organisations and the requirements of mentees. Below are some examples of the components involved in mentoring:

- Structure – mentoring can be an informal relationship between colleagues or friends, or a more formal arrangement organised by third party community projects, charities or educational establishments.

- Numbers – mentoring can be one-to-one or run in groups.

- Timescales – the frequency of sessions is down to individual and organisational commitments but is commonly on a monthly basis. The success of mentoring is vastly improved if the relationship is maintained over as long a period as possible.

- Mentor – a person with experience, time, empathy and a desire to help others to develop can be a mentor. Bridge Builder mentors are all middle and senior managers from large corporate organisations.

- Focus – this depends on the aim of the programme and includes, but is not limited to, academic performance, social skills, sporting development, personal development and career development.

The main purpose of mentoring is for the mentor to identify the goals of the mentee so that they may work together to solve problems and form action plans in order to achieve these goals. Mentors are committed to the needs of their mentee; the focus of mentoring sessions is always the mentee.

The focus of mentoring sessions is always the mentee.

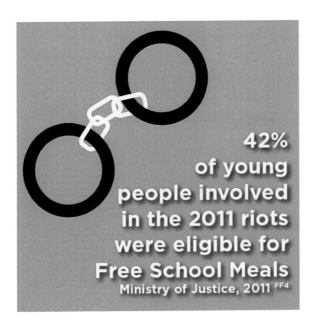

Clive Lewis

Businesses and Schools Working Together

'Education does two things. First, it teaches us how to make a living and second, it teaches us how to live.'

John Adams

The Bridge Builders Mentoring Scheme has excellent relationships with large corporate organisations which include community work and volunteering as part of their social responsibility policy. Volunteer mentors are recruited through these relationships, and are typically middle or senior managers, who have a wealth of experience to offer pupils. Our mentors are hand-picked for their enthusiasm, experience and commitment to making a difference to their mentees.

We are very grateful to Enterprise Rent-A-Car for partnering with Bridge Builders Mentoring since its inception. Enterprise Rent-A-Car is a global car rental company with over 68,000 employees, headquartered in Missouri, St. Louis. Mike Nigro, UK and Ireland Managing Director and Leigh Lafever-Ayer, Vice President of Human Resources, have worked tirelessly to help launch the programme. The business has supplied mentors, professional expertise and financial resources to assist in getting the initiative off the ground.

The practice of businesses and educational establishments working together is not a new one – as far back as the 16th century livery companies in the City were opening their own schools. However, there has been a recent recognition of the benefits inherent in such partnerships and an increase in the

The Bridge Builders Mentoring Scheme has excellent relationships with large corporate organisations which include community work and volunteering as part of their social responsibility policy.

Our mentors are hand-picked for their enthusiasm, experience and commitment to making a difference to their mentees.

The pairing of educational establishments with businesses dates back to the 16th century, and is very prevalent today.

availability and number of such schemes. In 2012, Barclays launched a scheme offering its support and expertise in a number of capacities to schools across England, and, in 2013, the UK Commission for Employment and Skills (UKCES) invested £2.4m to extend the reach of a programme called 'Business Class'. Other organisations exist to perform similar functions, particularly in areas where unemployment among young people is high – for example the Tower Hamlets EBP (Education Business Partnership) in London. And it is not just in the UK that such connections bear fruit – in March 2014, the Golden Apple awards in Kentuky, USA rewarded six companies for their business/education programmes, with the various programmes aiming to "build partnerships and increase communication between business and education in order to close skill gaps and increase the employability of high school graduates."

The Golden Apple awards in Kentucky, USA reward local companies' business/education programmes.

Long-running business/school partnerships benefit not only the mentee but also the mentor, the schools and businesses involved and the economy at large.

Benefits of Business/School partnerships

A successful and long-running business/school partnership not only benefits those directly associated with it (i.e. the mentor and mentee), but also has wider benefits for the schools and businesses involved, the local community and, when spread over a national level, the economy at large.

In their 2012 briefing paper, the UK Commission for Employment and Skills (UKCES) highlighted the following results from an independent study of their Business Class programme[5]:

- Participating schools highlighted a 38% improvement in academic achievement for students and a 25% improvement in the leadership and governance in participating schools.

- Schools and businesses involved in the evaluation of the Business Class programme thought that the programme had improved students' employability by over 40%.

- 26.1% of young people who could recall no contact with businesses whilst at school went on to become NEET (Not in Education, Employment, or Training). This reduced to 4.3% for those who had taken part in four or more activities involving businesses.

Young people involved in mentorship schemes tend to be more 'switched on' to learning through various activities with businesses.

Businesses often look more favourably at recruiting a young person who they know through direct engagement.

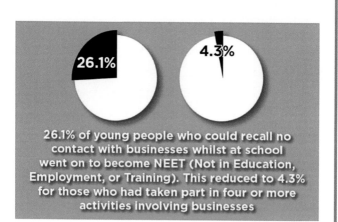

26.1% of young people who could recall no contact with businesses whilst at school went on to become NEET (Not in Education, Employment, or Training). This reduced to 4.3% for those who had taken part in four or more activities involving businesses

As well as these quantitative results, a number of qualitative benefits were also stated. For example, young people were said to be more 'switched on' to learning through various activities with businesses, partly because they could directly link their classroom learning with practical application in business. Businesses for their part said that they would look more favourably upon recruiting a young person who they knew through direct engagement as they saw them as having already shown an interest and enthusiasm in their company and the industry.

The positive effects of a successful mentor scheme have a long-lasting and wide reaching impact.

As is the case with the Golden Apple Awards in Kentucky, a key feature of the business/school partnership ethos is to close the gap between the skills employers want and the skills young people leave school with, something that these schemes are, naturally, very successful at doing. It is therefore easy to see how such partnerships have a knock-on effect, benefiting the student and the business simultaneously, which in turn benefits the school's performance and reputation, and has a positive impact on the community and the country at large. In short, there are a number of important winners in business/school partnerships and no losers.

The more contact students aged 14-19 have with employers in school, the less likely they are to become NEET aged 19-24

Education and Employers Taskforce, 2012[FF5]

Shamik Patel
Bridge Builders Mentor

Mike Nigro
MD - UK and Ireland - Enterprise Rent-A-Car

Utilising the Pupil Premium

'The value of college education is not the learning of many facts but training the mind to think.'

Albert Einstein

Schools normally fund work with Bridge Builders Mentoring through utilising the Pupil Premium. The Pupil Premium was introduced by the government in April 2011 as a means of raising the attainment of disadvantaged pupils and closing the gap between them and their peers. The 2014 Education Committee report cited earlier praised the Pupil Premium's efforts towards achieving this goal, stating:

> 'Policies such as the pupil premium...are to be welcomed as measures that could improve the performance of white working class children and increase attention on this group.'[6]

At the time of launch, three years before this report, a total budget of £625m was set aside and made available to publicly funded schools in England in order directly to assist children from low-income families who were eligible for free school meals, looked-after children and those from families with parents in the Armed Forces. The average amount of Pupil Premium funding received by all schools nationally in 2011–12 was £30,940 and the median was £19,520, with the amount per child at the time of launch being £488. The premium budget was increased to £1.25bn in 2012 and again in 2013 to £1.875bn (£900 per child). This figure will rise once more to £2.5bn in September 2014.

Schools normally fund work with Bridge Builders Mentoring through utilising the Pupil Premium.

The Pupil Premium was introduced in April 2011 as a means of raising the attainment of disadvantaged pupils and closing the gap between them and their peers.

The allocation of these funds by individual schools was left to the schools themselves, who were, it was decided, best placed to decide where the funds could best be used to achieve the goals of the Pupil Premium. A year after the launch, Ofsted conducted a study[7] into Pupil Premium usage among a number of participating schools. They found 14 different areas in which Pupil Premium funds were typically being used, with the most popular being the addition of new staff, but the second most popular area of spending was in one to one tuition – a key feature of mentoring.

Ofsted found that 1:1 tuition was second only to the acquisition of new staff in schools' Pupil Premium spending after the first year.

As well as one to one tuition being a popular avenue of Pupil Premium usage, the study also found that one in seven schools questioned reported using part or all of their Pupil Premium for mentoring. Bridge Builders has been at the forefront of this mentoring take-up, working with a number of schools using their Pupil Premium to fund the Bridge Builders Mentoring Scheme for their pupils.

The Ofsted report also found that 1 in 7 schools reported using part or all of their Pupil Premium for mentoring.

How does mentoring tie in with the aims of the Pupil Premium?

Having already outlined a number of key benefits to mentoring, and given the stated goal of the Pupil Premium (to 'raise the attainment of disadvantaged pupils'), it is important to illustrate how mentoring can help achieve this goal.

The previously mentioned Ofsted study states, the first year of the Pupil Premium saw one in seven schools utilising mentoring as a method of achieving their Pupil Premium goals. Whilst there is no overall data for the years to date, case studies (see the chapter at the end of this book) show that mentoring continues to be a very popular and effective method of bringing the target children up to the required standards in line with the aims of the Pupil Premium. The 2013 Sutton Trust Teaching and Learning Toolkit[8] had the following to say with regard to mentoring as a method of improving the attainment of disadvantaged pupils:

> 'There is some evidence that pupils from disadvantaged backgrounds are likely to benefit more (nearly double the impact). Other positive benefits have been reported in terms of attitudes to school, attendance and behaviour.
>
> Programmes which have a clear structure and expectation, provide training and support for mentors, and use mentors from a professional background, are associated with more successful outcomes.'

As we can see, mentoring has more of an impact precisely where it is required in terms of the Pupil Premium's chief goal. The report also states that community based programmes have a greater chance of success than solely school based ones, which backs up the Bridge Builders ideology of matching educational establishments with businesses in the community. One to one tuition and peer tutoring were also considered some of the most effective methods of improving attainment levels, two areas heavily linked to the mentoring process.

Mentoring continues to be a popular use of Pupil Premium spending and is an effective way of achieving the scheme's aims and objectives.

In 2013, The Sutton Trust praised the effect of mentoring programmes, especially for children from disadvantaged backgrounds.

The report also states that community based programmes have a greater chance of success than solely school based ones.

This is just the tip of the iceberg – an internet search for 'pupil premium mentoring' will reveal reports from dozens of schools from across the country detailing how they have operated their Pupil Premium mentoring schemes, ranging from appointing individual mentoring leaders to entire mentoring teams, or utilising the expertise of companies like Bridge Builders to run programmes for them.

An internet search for 'pupil premium mentoring' will reveal reports from dozens of schools from across the country detailing how they have operated their Pupil Premium mentoring schemes.

£2.5bn

The value of the Pupil Premium funding in 2014-15

Department of Education, 2014 [FF6]

Clive Lewis

Social Mobility

'He who opens a school door closes a prison.'

Victor Hugo

I was watching the film Smurfs 2 with my eight year old son the other day. I was struck by a line said by Papa to Smurfette in response to her feeling slightly inferior to others. He says "It doesn't matter where you were born. What matters is who you choose to be". How fitting that I should come across this powerful line whilst writing this book, and very relevant to the topic of social mobility.

Social mobility is a complex area. The UK government has attempted to address issues associated with it by introducing initiatives such as the Pupil Premium, which is touted as a means of improving social mobility. Social mobility is often associated with issues of class, but it is usually recognised as the movement of individuals or families within or between social strata and society.

The dictionary definition of social mobility is:

> The ability of individuals or groups to move within a social hierarchy with changes in income, education, occupation etc.[9]

In the past, in the UK, a person's position in society has often been fixed by, for example, birth, wealth, gender or ethnicity. The concern for social mobility is that people's position should not be fixed by these or any other factors. Everyone should have equal opportunity to succeed and fulfil their potential.

Social mobility is usually recognised as the movement of individuals or groups within or between the social hierarchies.

Bridge Builders Mentoring aims to improve social mobility and employability.

34

At Bridge Builders Mentoring we aim to improve social mobility and employability by helping young men from poor backgrounds realise their full potential. We provide the advice and guidance that many disadvantaged individuals lack for one reason or other. Too often, children from this bracket are not able to access the same advice and opportunities that their better off peers do, and this is a limiting factor on their future success, whatever their ambitions may be.

Our mentoring programme is an opportunity for these young men to learn from experienced individuals who have overcome a wide range of barriers in their own lives to become successful. It is a unique chance for the young men selected to have dedicated one-to-one attention from an adult outside of their school, family or social group, and gain a new perspective.

Every mentee is unique, but they all can learn a lot from their mentors.

Every one of our mentees is unique, with their own experiences, perceived barriers, beliefs and abilities. Any one of countlesss issues could be holding these young men back from achieving their best and potentially taking steps towards improving their lives. There is a lot for these young men to learn from their mentors. Bridge Builders mentors are business professionals, who show up on time, dress smartly and listen to their mentees. This commitment is incredibly powerful for the boys who are often battling to be heard and understood in a busy classroom, playground or at home. They learn that their voice and views are relevant, and this is an important step to empowering them to place value on themselves and their education.

Bridge Builders mentors are business professionals who show up on time, dress smartly and listen to their mentees.

Economic background is nothing to be ashamed of, nor is it a barrier to success.

Nobody should feel ashamed of their history or let it be a barrier to where they want to be in the future. Economic background should not, in a fair society, restrict the ability of any child forming, working towards or realising their goals. Bridge Builders Mentoring is working towards this for young men from poor backgrounds, so that they know how to apply themselves in the right way and work hard enough at it.

Empowering young men to achieve their fullest potential is a critical part of the programme. This has become a reality for me through a range of people helping to show me how, by taking a few small steps, I could begin to achieve my potential in a few areas of my life. Often, people are simply unaware of what actions can be taken to change their circumstances. Being frequently around people who are already excelling in a particular area increases the likelihood of inspiring someone to do something similar for themselves. The responsibility very much rests with each of us though. Philosopher Ray Waldo Emerson once said that *"We become what we think about all day long."*

Empowering young men to achieve their fullest potential is a critical part of the Bridge Builders Mentoring programme.

27%

The gap in educational attainment between FSM and non-FSM pupils

Department of Education, 2014 [FF7]

Employability

'Intelligence plus character – that is the goal of true
education.'

Martin Luther King

We at Bridge Builders realise that achieving our aims in
providing long-term, lasting difference to the lives of our
target demographic is about more than simply adjusting
their attitude towards different socio-economic groups.
They also need useful, practical advice about how to survive
in the world we would like them to inhabit, to build the skills
necessary to thrive in their new environment.

Our mentees need useful, practical advice about how to survive in the world we would like them to inhabit, to build the skills necessary to thrive in their new environment.

One of the most important things we want them to consider
in the long-term is their employability, to ensure that they
remain desirable in the workplace and desirous of success
within it. Throughout the course of their contact with our
mentors they will learn that there is a huge difference
between life within the education system and life in the
workplace. They will learn that the care, the attention and,
importantly, the multiple opportunities they are given
throughout their education swiftly come to an end in the
workplace and they take ultimate responsibility for their
own actions. This may be something that you and your
colleagues have tried to do, potentially on numerous
occasions, but the use of mentors from within the working
world gives more authenticity to this message. These
messages are delivered not as a short, sharp shock in the
first meeting but, as the process would suggest, carefully as
the bond between mentor and mentee is fostered – we

Throughout the course of their contact with our mentors they will learn that there is a huge difference between life within the education system and life in the workplace – the workplace is far less forgiving.

facilitate a careful transition between the educational world and the working world, our mentors imparting their knowledge of key attributes in any workplace such as honesty, reliability and flexibility, as well as learning how to treat colleagues and superiors in order initially to cement their place in the working world and then progress.

This facilitation is further enhanced by the work placements Bridge Builders offers as a mandatory part of the programme, allowing the mentees to gain invaluable experience in the working environment, something that they would normally find extremely hard to come by. We have already seen that many companies are more disposed to hiring individuals who have already undertaken a successful work placement with them, and so these work placements by themselves have the potential to be life changing, let alone the rest of the Bridge Builders programme. The programme as a whole in fact teaches participants an important lesson about life – the more they put into it, the more they will get out of it.

The economic case for employers

Work experience is a vital part of the transition from education into work. Lack of experience is the number one concern of British employers who have recruited young people but found them poorly prepared. This is the main reason employers turn away young applicants.

As of September 2012, work experience during Key Stage 4 is no longer compulsory, and the responsibility for careers guidance has been with individual schools and not local authorities. Since then, there have been varying levels of success recorded. New statutory guidelines issued in April

We facilitate a careful transition between the educational world and the working world.

This facilitation is further enhanced by the work placements Bridge Builders offers as a mandatory part of the programme.

The programme as a whole in fact teaches participants an important lesson about life – the more they put into it, the more they will get out of it.

Employers want young employees to be more prepared for work.

2014 clearly state that governing bodies are required to ensure that all pupils are provided with independent careers guidance, including a range of activities that might feature mentoring, coaching, careers fairs and work experience.

The importance of work experience is also consistently noted across a range of employer representative bodies in the United Kingdom, such as the Confederation of British Industry (CBI).

The UK Commission's largest employer survey has a sample size of around 90,000 establishments UK-wide, making it one of the largest and most comprehensive of its kind in the world. The Employer Skills Survey (ESS) provides detailed information at a sectoral and spatial level on the nature of recruitment and skills. In particular, it provides insights into which employers are struggling with skills gaps for their current staff and which are finding it difficult to recruit because of a lack of skills and/or experience among job applicants. It also provides a wealth of information on employers' views of the young people they have recruited into their first job upon leaving education, whether from school, college or university.

The most recent results from an Employer Skills Survey are from spring 2011[11]. This survey found that while only a minority of British employers (24%) had actually recruited a young person directly from education in the previous two to three years, the majority of those doing so found their new recruits well or very well prepared for work. Of those employers taking on graduates, 82% found them well or very

The UK Commission for Employment and Skills' Employer Skill Survey provides insights into which employers are struggling with skills gaps for their current staff and which are finding it difficult to recruit because of a lack of skills and/or experience among job applicants.

The ESS found that the majority of employers who recruited a young person directly from education found their new recruits well or very well prepared for work.

The figures decline as the age of the individual decreases.

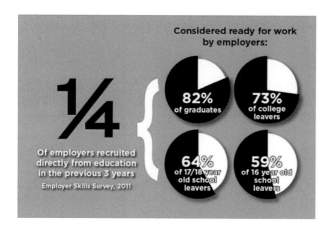

well prepared for work. This falls to 73% for those taking on 17/18-year-old college leavers, 64% of those taking on 17/18-year-old school leavers and 59% of those employers taking on 16-year-old school leavers.

These findings show the importance of work experience to employers.

Survey findings show that the importance of work experience to employers when recruiting cannot be understated and, as would be expected, the impact of experience of the workplace on the labour market outcomes of young people later on are clear. In December 2011, the Department for Education (DfE) published research[12] that used the Labour Force Survey and the Longitudinal Survey of Young People in England (LSYPE) to look at how transitions into work varied for different groups of young people. This research found that young learners who combined work with their studies at age 16/17 were more likely to be in work later on and earn more than those who did not.

In 2011 the Department for Education found that young learners who combined work with their studies at age 16 and/or 17 were more likely to be in work later on and earn more than those who did not.

Given the premium attached to work experience and persistent problems with youth employment, there is a real need to improve access to work experience.

In summary, employers think that experience is vital when recruiting; young people and teachers alike want more opportunities; and it is a clear aim of government policy (in England). However, establishing more high-quality work experience opportunities is contingent on employers engaging with education and supplying the places. The Bridge Builders Scheme fills this gap.

Employers think that experience is vital when recruiting; young people and teachers alike want more opportunities; and it is a clear aim of government policy.

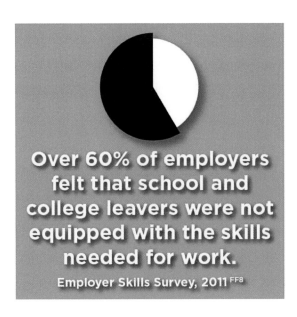

Over 60% of employers felt that school and college leavers were not equipped with the skills needed for work.

Employer Skills Survey, 2011 [FF8]

Character and Resilience

'Education is an ornament in prosperity

and a refuge in adversity.'

Aristotle

Earlier in this handbook I gave examples of my experiences of engaging with youngsters entering the world of work. There is a growing body of research linking social mobility to social and emotional skills including empathy, ability to make and retain relationships, resilience, delayed gratification and control. Character is important. Examples of what such traits might resemble include:

- Belief in one's ability to achieve

- Understanding the relationship between effort and reward

- Patience to pursue long term goals

- Perseverance to stick with the task at hand

- Ability to bounce back in the face of adversity

It is easy to become confused as to what employers really want, or will do in the future.

In a world of qualifications, training and transferable skills, it is easy to become confused as to what employers really want, or will do in the future. According to a 2011 survey by national recruitment consultancy firm Reed[13], 96% of the 1,263 organisations questioned said they would rather hire someone without the complete skillset but with the right mindset over the alternative. So if skills alone won't get you the job, what will? What is it that employers are looking for?

The right mindset is more likely to get you hired than possessing a complete skillset.

The answer is 'values' – the core traits that come together to make up an individual's attitude to their work. Character and resilience are critical in this regard. Employers are looking for candidates with the right skillset and the right mindset – in other words they want someone with the tools to do the job and drive to get it done on time and professionally. Most important to employers is a strong work ethic. This doesn't just mean working hard, it also means working smart. Prospective employers will want to see that young people have the drive to see tasks through to the end, that they take pride in what they do and work intelligently and within constraints of time and money.

Linked to work ethic is teamwork – an essential value in almost any workplace, in any industry. Individuals who can demonstrate that they are team players, that they are prepared to offer support, receive advice and work with their team to achieve common goals, will be highly regarded. It may be a cliché to say that someone is a team player, but it is an important one to remember and demonstrate.

Employers are looking for 'values' - the core traits that come together to make up an individual's attitude to their work.

They want someone with the tools to do the job and drive to get it done on time and professionally.

Most important is a strong (and smart) work ethic.

The next most important value is teamwork.

Skills employers are looking for:

Employers will also want to be sure of any prospective employee's dependability and responsibility. They will want to know that they will be somewhere when they say they'll be there and that the young person won't shirk from the responsibility of their position when things get difficult or if they fall behind schedule. This relates back to basic issues of character and resilience and indeed trust, the foundations upon which relationships are built.

Employers will also want to be sure of any prospective employee's dependability and responsibility.

Those with a positive attitude are also favoured by employers, perhaps for obvious reasons; someone with a positive attitude will approach a problem and see how it can be overcome, whereas someone with a negative attitude might let the first setback be the last.

A positive outlook is a trait also favoured by employers.

Professionalism is also a key value employers look for. Professionals look, dress and speak in a manner reflecting their profession, company and personal pride.

Employers also want professionalism.

Another study that reinforced the idea of traits and values being more important than skills was conducted in 2011 by IBM[14]. They questioned 1709 CEOs around the world and asked them what they looked for when recruiting staff. The results were, in order of importance:

1. Collaborative

2. Communicative

3. Creative

4. Flexible

5. Opportunity seeking

A study of over 1000 CEOs put character traits above any individual skills in terms of importance to them.

As the results show, the CEOs put character traits above any individual skills in terms of importance to them and the success of their organisations. Looking at those traits, it is hard to believe that they have altered hugely in the last ten to fifteen years or are likely to change in the near future, unless there is a seismic shift in industry.

Character traits are rated highly amongst employers.

Here is an example of the importance of this area. Recently I heard of a story of a school boy who is an excellent footballer. At 14, he is already playing at county level. However, he has some work to do on building his character and resilience. His coach was giving him some advice which he didn't agree with. His response was to shout at the coach and walk off the training pitch. The coach will not let him back until he apologises for his behaviour. He is refusing to do this. He is now jeopardising a promising footballing career for allowing his pride to get in the way of acknowledging that his coach has the right of duty to provide constructive feedback in this stage in his career.

Etiquette Skills

'It is not what is poured into a student that counts but what is planted.'

Linda Conway

Of the five training programmes run by Bridge Builders, Etiquette Skills is the most popular by far. As many of us know, etiquette is a critical area concerning those from poor socio-economic backgrounds. As we have touched on already, the young men who could gain the most from Bridge Builders tend to be the ones who, for a number of reasons, have had very little exposure to the kind of social group they will commonly find in the workplace; they would feel just as out of place dumped into the middle of the office as many of us would be if we were dumped into an inner city housing estate. They are often ill-equipped to deal appropriately with authority figures and many need basic guidance in terms of working harmoniously with colleagues, especially given that almost every office contains a handful of people who are not the easiest to get along with, regardless of one's socio-economic background.

Knowledge of basic manners is, as we all have experienced in our lives, not something with which everyone is imbued, and this is especially the case with our target demographic for whom showing politeness and good manners in their daily activities is sometimes far from the top of their list of priorities. There is a very serious side to this however, as the knock on effect means that when they have to deal with an authority figure of importance to them, for example an

Of the four training programmes run by Bridge Builders, Etiquette Skills is the most popular by far.

Many of the young men we target are ill equipped to deal properly with authority figures.

Many need basic guidance in terms of working harmoniously with colleagues.

Politeness and good manners are not often instilled in our target demographic.

interviewer for a job, they simply do not know how to go about it professionally and politely. Given the swathes of young people currently seeking work, including many with a university education, employers are able to cherry pick the best candidates, and such a fundamental disadvantage as not knowing how to address a potential employer ensures that these candidates will almost certainly be overlooked. It is important that they realise that people remember those they have had pleasant dealings with and vice versa, something that can be so powerful and yet so easy to achieve.

Employers are able to cherry pick the best candidates, and such a fundamental disadvantage as not knowing how to address a potential employer spells disaster.

In his bestselling book *Emotional Intelligence*[15], psychologist Daniel Goleman claims that EQ (emotional intelligence) is more important than IQ, both to individuals and businesses. Our level of EQ, he says, dictates our ability to deal with both ourselves and other people over four domains – self-awareness, self-management, empathy and social skills – and that these skills matter more than simply how clever we are. He states that schools introducing EQ programmes aimed at teaching values associated with etiquette, manners and the like have as a result experienced lower anti-social behaviour and higher pro-social behaviour and academic achievement, leading to his belief that EQ should be taught in all schools to give young people the perfect grounding for dealing with other people in a variety of situations whilst also having faith and convictions in their own beliefs. This philosophy is certainly something that Bridge Builders bears in mind, and indeed we run a social skills and etiquette course that covers a number of areas in this field, including:

Daniel Goleman, author of the bestselling Emotional Intelligence, promotes EQ (emotional intelligence) over IQ.

Our EQ is our self-awareness, self-management, empathy and social skills – they matter more than our intelligence.

- First impressions

- 'Please' and 'thank you'

- Acknowledging others

- Punctuality

- Etiquette in communication

- Use of language (written and verbal)

- Effective listening

This is just a selection of the modules on the course which is run over one day and features engaging, memorable activities that will offer the foundations that participants can build on in order to ensure that they have the EQ required to prosper both in the workplace and in the wider world.

Case Studies

Louis and Paul

Louis is 14 and in Year 9. Things at home over the last few years have been tough; his mum is a single parent, dad is not around and his grandfather, the only constant adult male in his life, passed away recently. Louis is a really bright boy with a lot of common sense but is often absent and, when he is in class, frequently disruptive. He has been identified as dyslexic but refuses to engage with his teachers about how this might be addressed.

Louis was chosen to take part in the Bridge Builders Mentoring programme because his teachers hope that the opportunity for him to have one to one focus from an external adult male would give him a new perspective and perhaps a new role model. Paul was assigned as Louis' mentor. He immediately found Louis to be a friendly, likeable young man, and they found a common interest in their love of motorbikes.

During the first couple of mentoring sessions, Paul let Louis do most of the talking, sharing some of his own experiences where appropriate to build rapport with Louis. Before the third session, one of Louis' teachers informed Paul that Louis had been put under temporary exclusion measures the week before, as a result of "kicking off" at his English teacher. Paul suspected this might be related to Louis' literacy difficulties and felt that, at this stage, he had a good enough relationship with Louis to gently ask him about it.

Louis admitted that he had always found reading and writing hard, and it frustrated and embarrassed him. It made him feel stupid to be so slow, and he had decided that he wasn't interested in learning anymore – he was going to be a mechanic and didn't need to know about Shakespeare to do that.

This was an important piece of information. It was great that Louis had ambition, but Paul suspected that literacy skills would be very necessary if Louis was to achieve these goals. Prior to the next session, Paul spent some time researching and talking to teachers, finding out about mechanics courses in the area. He found out that the vocational courses that Louis would be interested in would include further study of GCSE English and mathematics to achieve at least a C, if he didn't achieve these at school.

Paul relayed these findings to Louis. Louis said he'd been told this before – but assumed that it was just his English and maths teachers trying to trick him! Paul explored further how English and maths might be beneficial in mechanics, and suggested that Louis might want to accept some of the extra help that he was being offered. Seeing the point of accepting he needed to improve from a new angle, Louis agreed to take on the extra help. At a later date, Paul also arranged for Louis to get some work experience at a local garage, so he could build his CV and develop his employability skills.

Louis and Paul are going to continue their sessions into Louis' next year at school, to help maintain focus as he begins his GCSE studies.

Jonah and Al

Jonah is 16 and in his final year of GCSE study. He is a keen rugby player, and his school has a policy of using some of the Pupil Premium funding to enable students eligible for Free School Meals, as Jonah is, to participate fully in extra-curricular activities, for example subsidising kit and travel expenses. However, all participation in sport outside PE classes is conditional on behaviour, attendance and attainment.

Jonah was initially selected for the Bridge Builders Mentoring programme in September because he expressed an interest following a training skills course on employability skills. He went to sessions and engaged with his mentor Al, talking about his plans to become a rugby coach. However, in the December and January sessions, Al noticed that Jonah was increasingly disengaged and seemed to be very tired.

In February's session, Jonah was very animated. He had been dropped from the rugby team because his attainment and performance had been slipping, and been given a detention for "mouthing off" at the coach. Al asked what had changed in the last couple of months. Jonah said he was trying really hard to do everything and he had taken on extra shifts at his leisure centre job to get more experience and earn money for a moped. It turned out he was working there all day Saturday, and also on Monday, Wednesday and Thursday evenings.

Al raised the question with Jonah: when was he doing his homework? Jonah mumbled that he wasn't really, he was too busy and when he had nights off he was either rugby training or too tired to do anything – but he was still trying hard in class. Al put it to him that actually Jonah was burning the candle at both ends. He advised Jonah that he had once been in a similar situation – whilst at university, he had been working part-time at a bar to save up for his gap year. He had found it difficult to say no to shifts and ended up so tired he was falling asleep in lectures. Not only that – his final year project partner was upset with him as he kept being late and was not contributing to the project.

Al told Jonah that he had had to talk to his manager at the bar and explain that he needed to reduce his number of shifts until after his project was complete – he also had to apologise to his partner and tutor for letting them down. He didn't lose his job, his manager was very understanding, and his partner and tutor accepted his apology. He was able to get enough rest to put everything into his final months at university. Had he not done that, he might not have achieved the 2:1 grade he needed to get on the graduate programme that started his career.

So, Jonah realised that, although he really wanted a moped now, he was putting his rugby, education and career prospects at risk. He only had a few months left of GCSEs, he could delay saving for his moped until the summer when he had more time to work. Al advised that he should probably apologise to his rugby coach too, as he might need him as a reference to get onto the college course he wanted to do after GCSEs.

Jonah and Al finished their mentoring relationship just before exams, but in the couple of months between, Jonah reduced his shifts at work and did some catch up revision lessons with teachers to get him back on track for his exams.

David and Jeff

David is 17 and is in his first year of catering college, much of which is down to Jeff, his mentor. Jeff is an advertising executive for a global supermarket chain and has experience in the mentoring arena having raised a foster child of his own for fifteen years. David was introduced to Bridge Builders after a number of issues that had plagued his school career magnified in his final, critical GCSE year. David had a history of bad behaviour, primarily truancy and verbal abuse of teachers. He was frequently sent out of class and was suspended from school three times. Switching schools had no effect and he was in danger of leaving school with no qualifications.

David lived at home with his mother and younger brother, their father having abandoned them when David was just three years old. His mother was often also on the receiving end of David's verbal barrages, although underneath this he was fiercely loyal to her. She had taken David to counselling a year previously, where it had been identified that David's problem was in taking instructions, but no further progress had been made.

Jeff and David were paired for their shared passion for food and cooking. On their third meeting Jeff brought in a home cooked lunch to share, and found that David was very keen to learn about the ingredients in it and the methods of cooking. Jeff casually entered into conversations with David about his reactions to giving orders, discovering that he often took a simple request out of context and made the teacher seem much more controlling than they actually were. Jeff urged him to take deep breaths and consider what was being asked of him in such situations before reacting. Jeff also looked into catering courses for David, finding a catering college nearby. He informed David of the courses and the qualifications he needed to enrol, also informing David's mother of the suggestion. Through a careful combined effort they persuaded him to try for an NVQ, with Jeff and David's meetings taking on a culinary showcase as Jeff brought an ever wider variety of meals to the meetings. These helped keep David focused and gave him something to look forward to in the short term while also keeping him focused on the long term goal.

David sat his GCSEs and achieved the required grades to qualify for catering college, where his first two terms have passed with great success. Jeff and David are still in contact, and David occasionally cooks for Jeff!

Tre and Sam

Tre is a 16-year-old boy who lives with his mother and father on an estate in North London. His parents have a fractious relationship and Tre used to find solace away from their fighting through football, both playing and watching his favourite team, Tottenham Hotspurs. When he turned 15, Tre's mother noticed that his interest in football had suddenly waned which coincided with a drop in his performance at school, especially concerning his attention span, levels of interest and fatigue – he always seemed tired. He was also much more withdrawn and spent greater amounts of time by himself. His mother tried to talk to him about the situation but he simply said he didn't care about football any more and that school was boring, even the subjects he had previously shown aptitude for. His performance at school deteriorated to the point where the headmistress herself became personally involved in his case, and once all usual methods had been exhausted Bridge Builders became involved, with Tre at risk from being suspended.

Tre was paired with Sam, a 36-year-old middle manager for a construction firm and former West Ham youth footballer. Sam used his footballing background and the fact that he was a fan of Tottenham Hotspurs' rival team Arsenal to rekindle some of the fire in Sam that Tre's mother said he used to posses. The first two sessions didn't yield much, with Tre his usual defensive, sullen self, but on the third session Sam brought a football and the session ended in a kick-about in the school car park, with Tre showing great enthusiasm for Sam's skills and asking how to perform certain tricks. This was the breakthrough Sam was looking for, and it was clear that the issue was not with football itself. Sam, the headteacher and Sam's mother agreed that if they could crack this disillusionment with his favourite sport then it would have a positive effect all round.

Sam spent two more football-themed sessions with Tre, using the privacy of the school gym and the distraction of playing football to try and get to the root of the problem.

On the fourth session the truth was finally revealed – Tre had been bullied during football training for his weekend club team because of his height (he was shorter than average with a slight frame), with two of the bullies attending his school. It was quickly clear that this bullying had caused the negative impact on his schooling and the depression he had slipped into. This was the information everyone involved in Tre's interests had been waiting for. Whilst the school took their own steps in dealing with the situation, Sam prepared a video montage of some of the best footballers throughout history of Tre's height or shorter. Tre greatly enjoyed this and it had an immediate impact on his confidence levels. Two weeks later he had signed for a different football team and had expressed a desire to change position from striker to winger, a change which suited his slighter frame and fast speed. He was an instant success in his new role for his new team, which, together with the school's successful dealing with the bullying situation, led to him being pulled back from the brink as far as his education went. He even signed up for the school football team, eventually playing in the same team as the two former bullies.

Tre's mentoring had an unexpected effect too – his father began to play a more active role in Tre's life, taking him to a couple of Tottenham Hotspur games and taking much more interest in his education. In this case Sam's clever thinking in regards to approaching the sessions paid dividends, something that would not have happened without Bridge Builders' intervention.

Conclusion

Throughout its history, Bridge Builders has begun to change the lives of dozens of young men who, sometimes through little fault of their own, are at very high risk of slipping through the cracks in society and ending up in a place where the way out can be almost impossible to find on their own. We have provided a guiding light to help them find their way out and given them the opportunity to inhabit a world they would have not previously considered was open to them. Many of these young men have left our courses empowered, confident and ready to take the first step towards living a happy, successful and, importantly for them, legal, life. I hope this book has succeeded in transmitting the pride we at Bridge Builders have in our scheme and the results that they achieve.

I also hope that this book has succeeded in doing justice to the enormously positive impact of the cornerstone of the Bridge Builders approach – mentoring. I have seen many times just how effective mentoring can be in transforming disinterested and unmotivated young men into highly enthusiastic and confident individuals who are eager to learn, work and achieve. At a practical level, having someone on the 'inside' who can help shed some myths about the factors involved in becoming upwardly mobile (finding a job, the importance of education etc.) is incredibly helpful, given that the chances of them coming across this information independently is very unlikely. More important however is the emotional impact of mentoring. On many occasions I have seen mentors become more than role models to these young men – I have seen them become the father figures many of them never had when growing up. I was lucky enough to grow up with two parents, which is something not experienced by a growing number of our target group. Having someone who encourages them but at the same time commands respect and fosters a desire in the participants to seek their appreciation is a very powerful motivational tool. Of course this does not happen in every case, but I'm sure you can think of a number of pupils who are lacking just that sort of role model in their lives.

As well as our record in mentoring, I would also advocate the Bridge Builders method because of our track record in enlisting the help of local businesses in the schemes we run. This approach only increases the chance of a successful outcome to the placement and gives the participant even more motivation to succeed, especially if they particularly take to the company in question, which happens on many occasions.

I would like to conclude this book by asking that, whether you believe Bridge Builders is the strategy for you or not, you seriously consider a mentoring scheme for your most at-risk young men. Of course I would be delighted if you did choose Bridge Builders, but one-to-one mentoring, when done properly of course, is a proven winner when it comes to turning around the lives of the young men who might otherwise find the light at the end of the tunnel extinguished.

Thank you for reading, and I wish you success.

Clive Lewis

References

[1] Big Brothers Big Sisters (2012) *Big Brothers Big Sisters' Youth Outcome Report – Executive Summary.* Available from: http://www.bbbs.org/atf/cf/%7B8778D05C-7CCB-4DEE-9D6E-70F27C016CC9%7D/012412_YOS_executive.pdf. Last accessed 30.07.2014.

[2] Joseph Rowntree Foundation (2012). *Can Changing Aspirations and Attitudes Impact on Education Attainment? A Review of Interventions.* Available from: http://www.jrf.org.uk/sites/files/jrf/education-attainment-interventions-full.pdf. Last accessed 30.07.2014.

[3] Gutman, L.M., Schoon, I. (2013) *The impact of non-cognitive skills on outcomes for young people: Literature review.* Available from: http://educationendowmentfoundation.org.uk/uploads/pdf/Non-cognitive_skills_literature_review.pdf. Last accessed 30.07.2014

[4] Cinncinati.com (2014) *Celebrating education.* Available from: http://www.cincinnati.com/story/news/local/2014/04/24/celebrating-education-northern-kentucky/8089411/. Last accessed 30.07.2014.

[5] UKCES (2012) *Business and Schools: Building the World of Work Together.* Available from: http://dera.ioe.ac.uk/14139/1/business-and-schools-building-the-world-of-work-together.pdf. Last accessed: 30.07.2014.

[6] House of Commons Education Committee (2014). *Underachievement in Education by White Working Class Children.* HC 142 Incorporating HC 727, Session 2013-14. House of Commons London: The Stationery Office Limited

[7] OFSTED (2012). *The Pupil Premium: How Schools are using the Pupil Premium Funding to Raise Achievement for Disadvantaged Pupils.* Available from http://www.ofsted.gov.uk/sites/default/files/documents/surveys-and-good-practice/t/The%20Pupil%20Premium.pdf. Last accessed 30.07.2014.

[8] Sutton Trust (2013). *Sutton Trust – EEF Teaching and Learning Toolkit.* Available from: http://educationendowmentfoundation.org.uk/uploads/toolkit/Teaching_and_Learning_Toolkit_(Spring_2013).pdf. Last accessed 30.07.2014.

[9] "social mobility." *Dictionary.com.* 2014. http://www.dictionary.reference.com. Last accessed 30.07.2014.

[10] Blanden et al. (2005) *Intergenerational Mobility in Europe and North America.* Available from: http://cep.lse.ac.uk/about/news/IntergenerationalMobility.pdf. Last accessed 30.07.2014.

[11] UKCES (2012). *UK Commission's Employer Skills Survey 2011: UK Results.* Available from: https://www.gov.uk/government/uploads/system/uploads/attachment_data/file/303374/ukces-employer-skills-survey-11.pdf. Last accessed 30.07.2014.

[12] Crawford et al. (2011) *Young People's Education and Labour Market Choices Aged 16/17 to 18/19.* Available from: http://dera.ioe.ac.uk/13624/1/DFE-RR182.pdf. Last accessed 30.07.2014.

[13] James Reed, Paul G Stoltz (2013). *Put Your Mindset to Work: The One Asset You Really Need to Win and Keep the Job You Love.* London: Penguin.

[14] Kevin Kruse (2012). *Top 4 Traits of "Future Proof" Employees, According to 1,709 CEOs*. Available: http://www.forbes.com/sites/kevinkruse/2012/12/26/ibm-ceo-study/. Last accessed 06.01.2014.

[15] Daniel Goleman (1996). *Emotional Intelligence: Why it can Matter More Than IQ*. London: Bloomsbury.

Fast Fact References

FF1 Lord et al. (2013) *Pupils not Claiming Free School Meals: 2013 Research Report.* Available from: https://www.gov.uk/government/uploads/system/uploads/attachment_data/file /266339/DFE-RR319.pdf. Last accessed 30.07.2014.

FF2 Jerrim, J. (2013). *The Reading Gap: The socio-economic gap in children's reading skills: a cross-national comparison using PISA 2009.* Available from: http://www.suttontrust.com/news/publications/the-reading-gap/readinggap.pdf. Last accessed 30.07.2014.

FF3 Department for Education (2014). *GCSE and equivalent attainment by pupil characteristics in England: 2012 to 2013.* Available from: https://www.gov.uk/government/uploads/system/uploads/attachment_data/file /280689/SFR05_2014_Text_FINAL.pdf. Last accessed 30.07.2014.

FF4 Berman, G (2011). *The August 2011 Riots: A Statistical Summary.* Available from: http://www.parliament.uk/briefing-papers/SN06099.pdf. Last accessed 30.07.2014.

FF5 Education and Employers (2012). *It's Who You Meet: Why Employer Contacts at School Make a Difference to the Employment Prospects of Young Adults.* Available from: http://www.educationandemployers.org/wp-content/uploads/2014/06/its_who_you_meet_final_26_06_12.pdf. Last accessed 30.07.2014.

FF6 Department for Work and Pensions (2014). *Child Poverty Strategy 2014-2017.* Available from: https://www.gov.uk/government/uploads/system/uploads/attachment_data/file /324103/Child_poverty_strategy.pdf. Last accessed 30.07.2014.

FF7 Department for Education (2014). *GCSE and equivalent attainment by pupil characteristics in England: 2012 to 2013.* Available from: https://www.gov.uk/government/uploads/system/uploads/attachment_data/file /280689/SFR05_2014_Text_FINAL.pdf. Last accessed 30.07.2014.

FF8 CBI and The Pearson Think Tank (2012). *CBI/Pearson Education and Skills Survey 2012: Learning to Grow: what employers need to learn from education and skills.* Available from: http://creative-blueprint.co.uk/policy/item/cbi-pearson-education-and-skills-survey-2012#sthash.3LGeaFK8.dpuf. Last accessed 30.07.2014.

FF9 Department for Education (2013). *Destinations of Key Stage 4 and Key Stage 5 Pupils, 2010/2011.* Available from: https://www.gov.uk/government/uploads/system/uploads/attachment_data/file /224721/Destinations_Characteristics_SFR_FINAL.pdf. Last accessed 30.07.2014.

FF10 Department for Education (2011). *A Profile of Pupil Absence in England.* Available from: https://www.gov.uk/government/uploads/system/uploads/attachment_data/file /183445/DFE-RR171.pdf. Last accessed 30.07.2014.